MAGICAL FAIRY TALE

Coloring Books For Adults Inspiration and Stress Relief

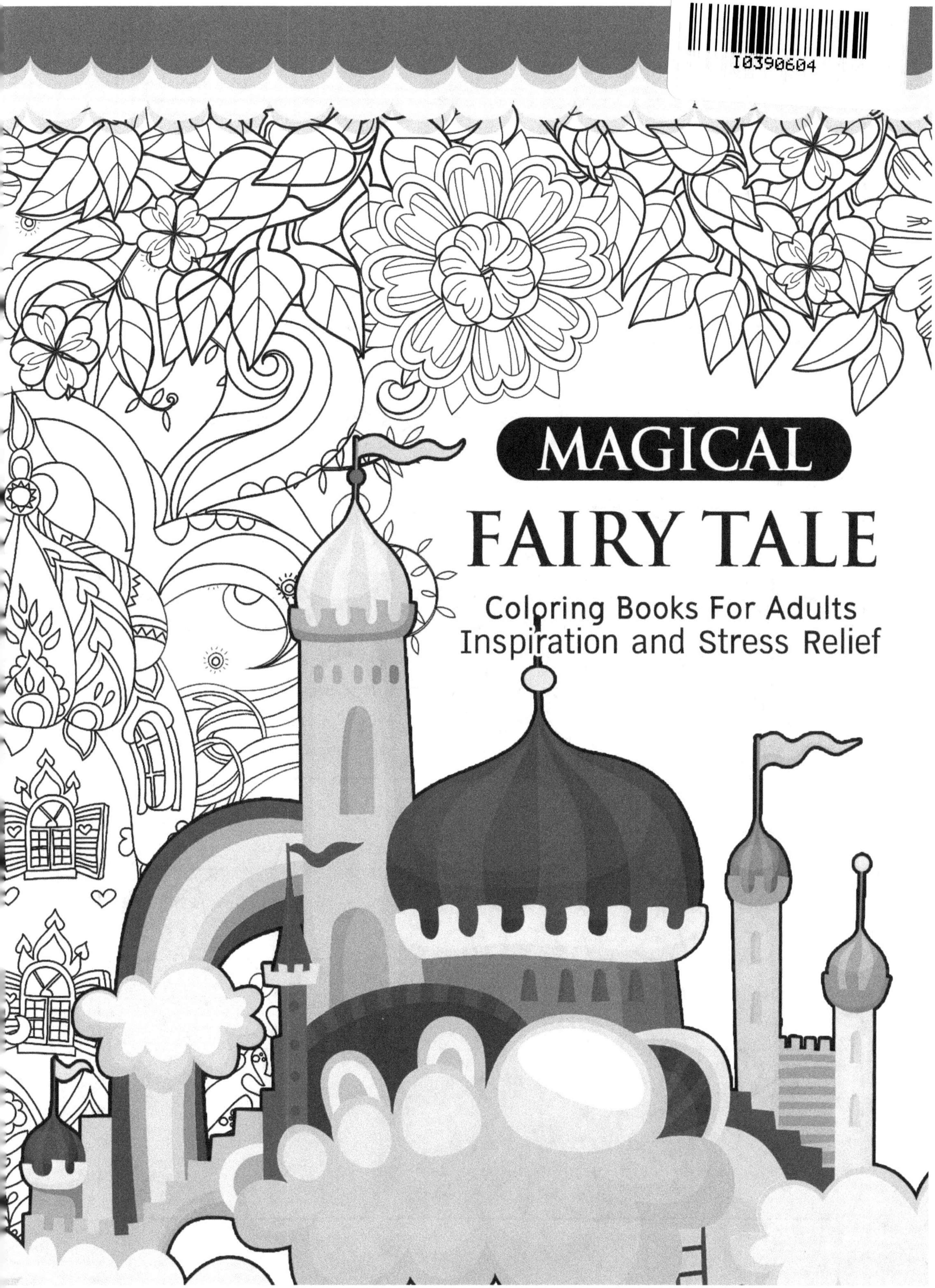

TEST YOUR COLOR

TEST YOUR COLOR

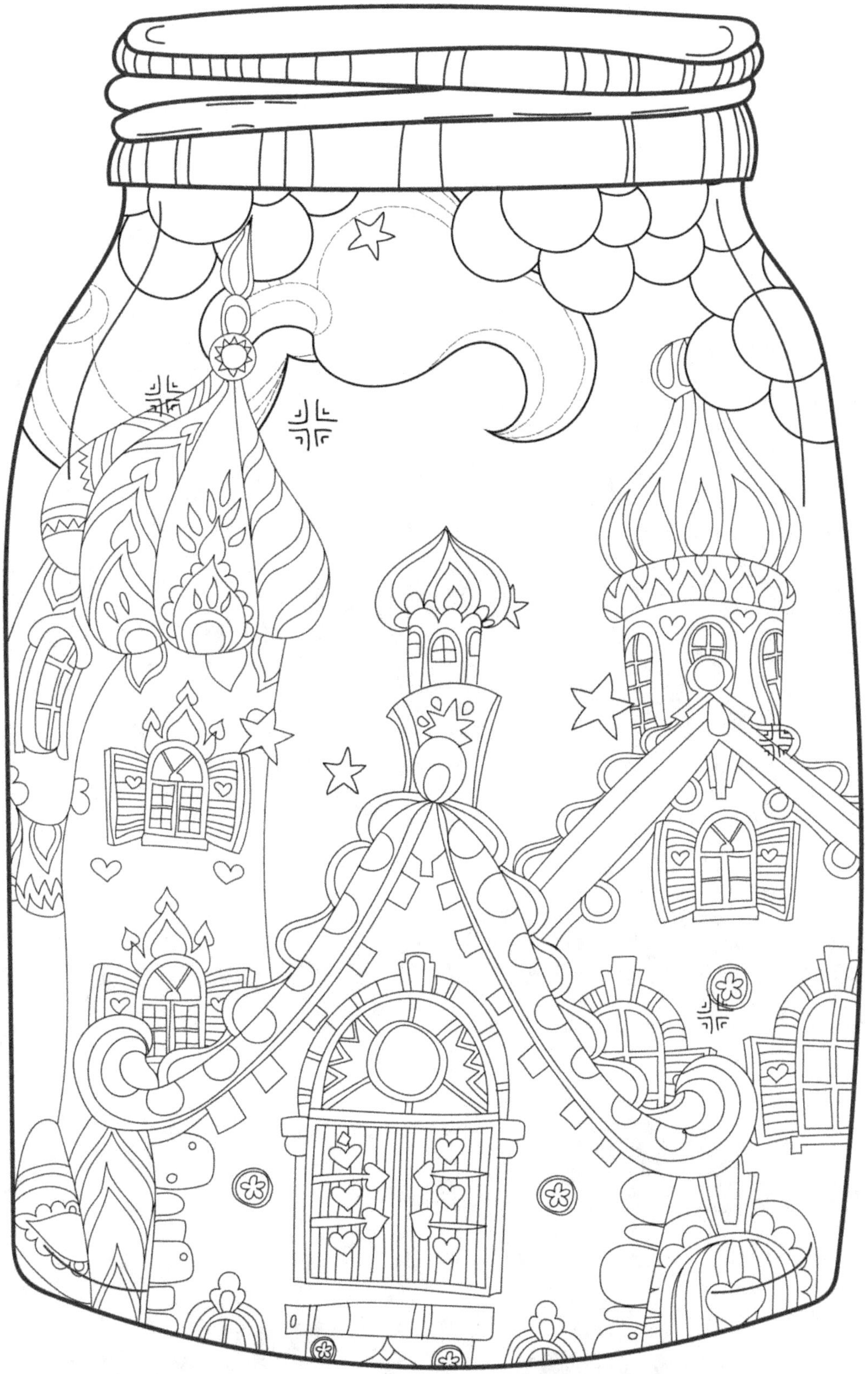

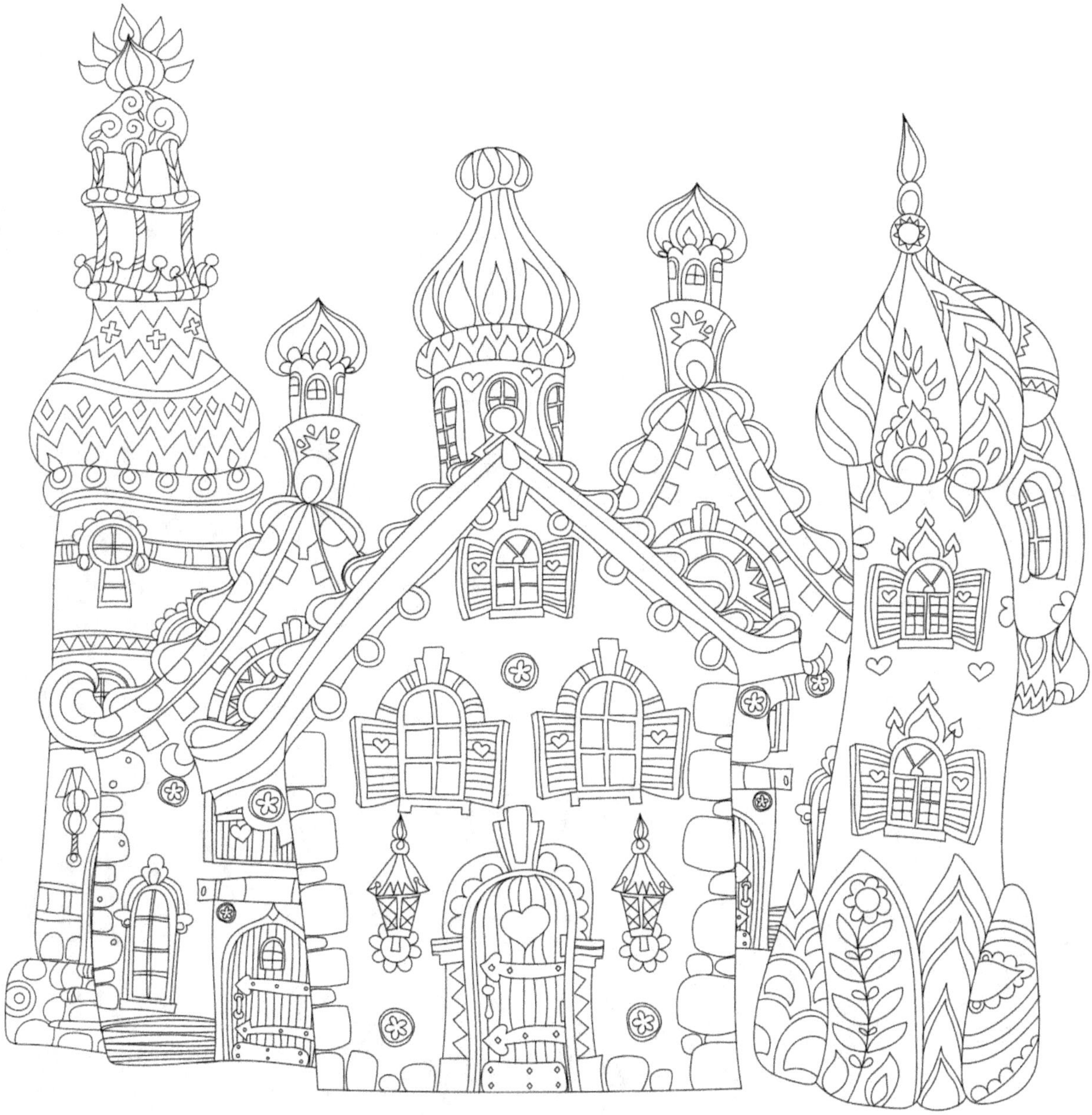

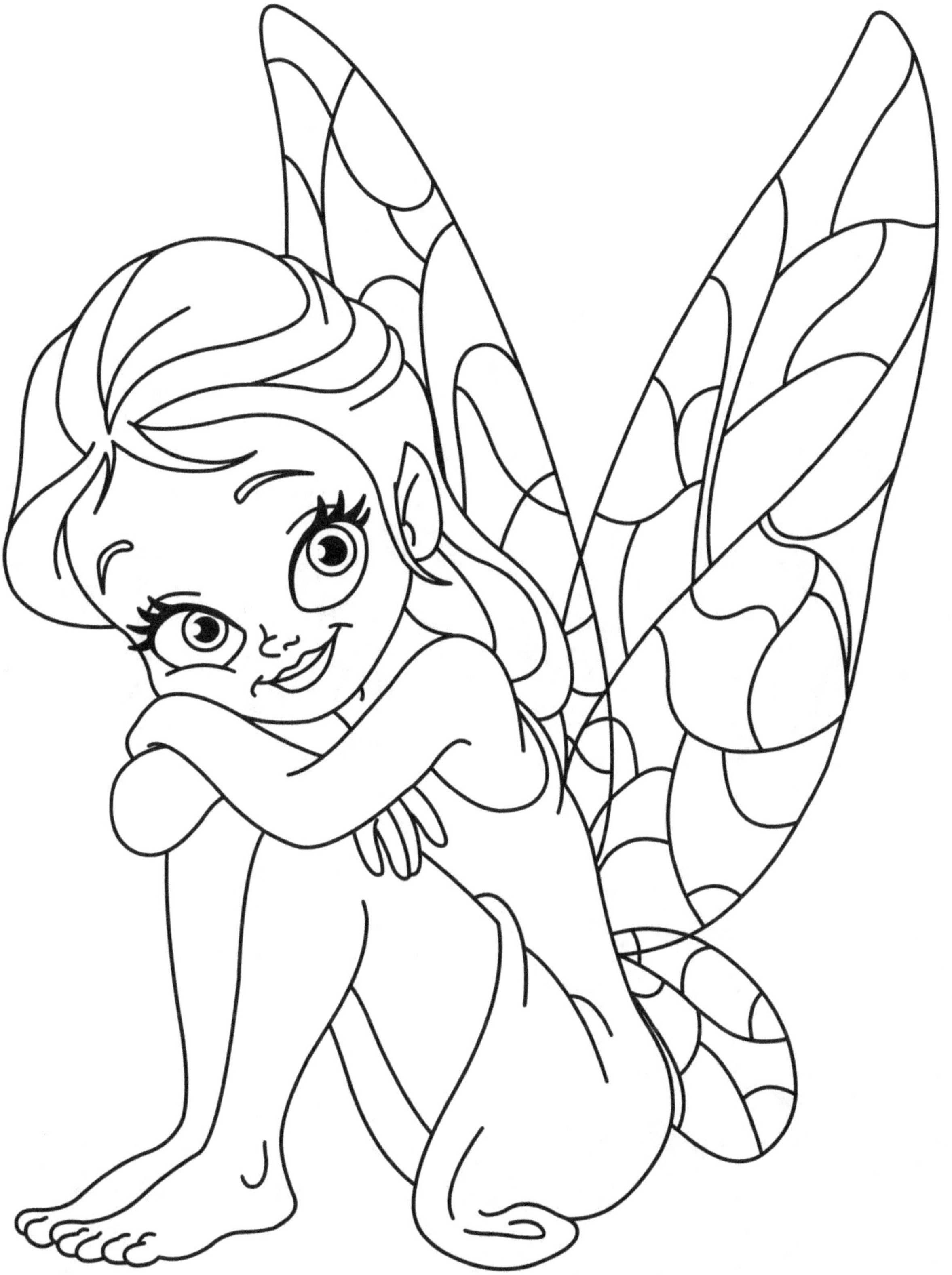

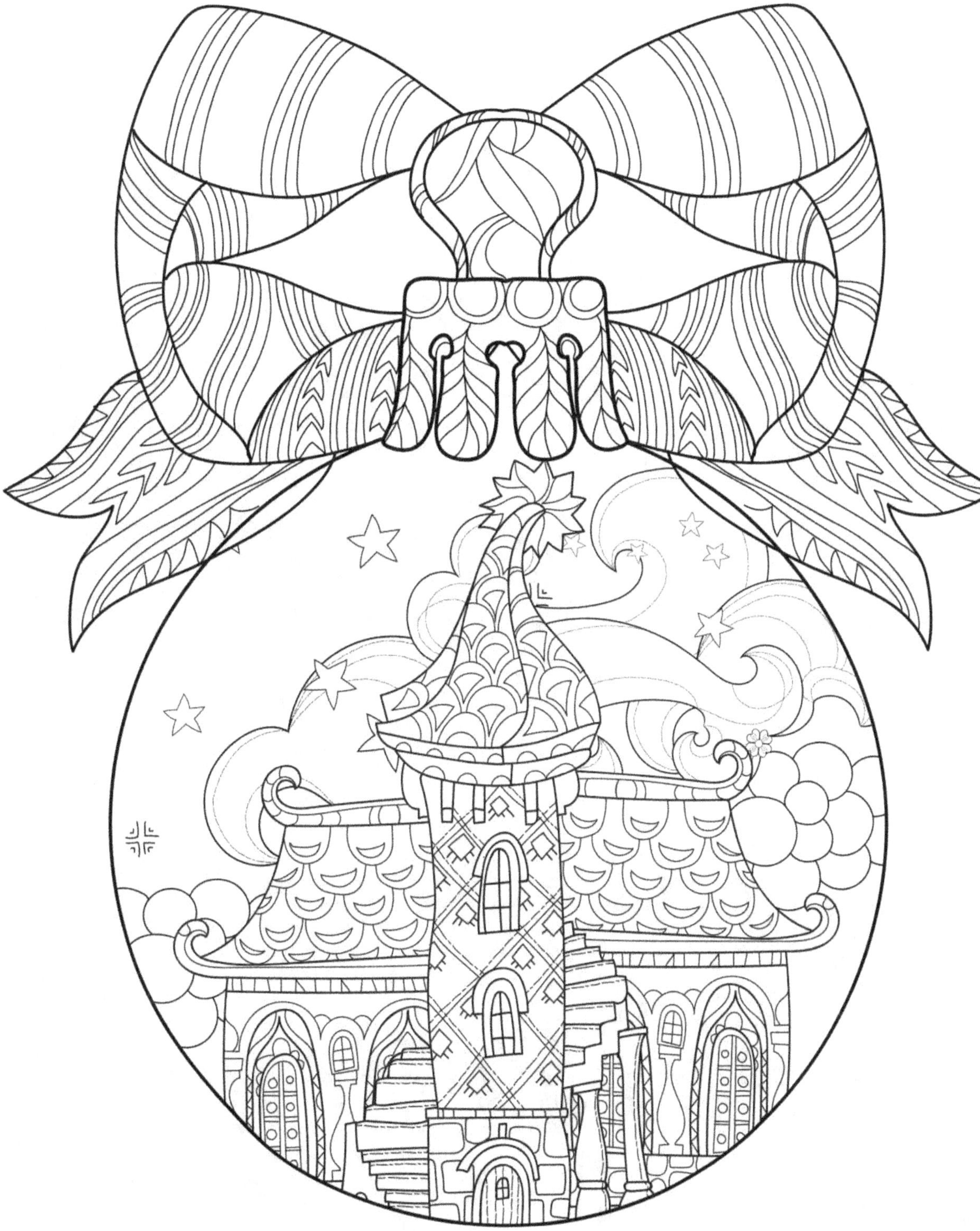

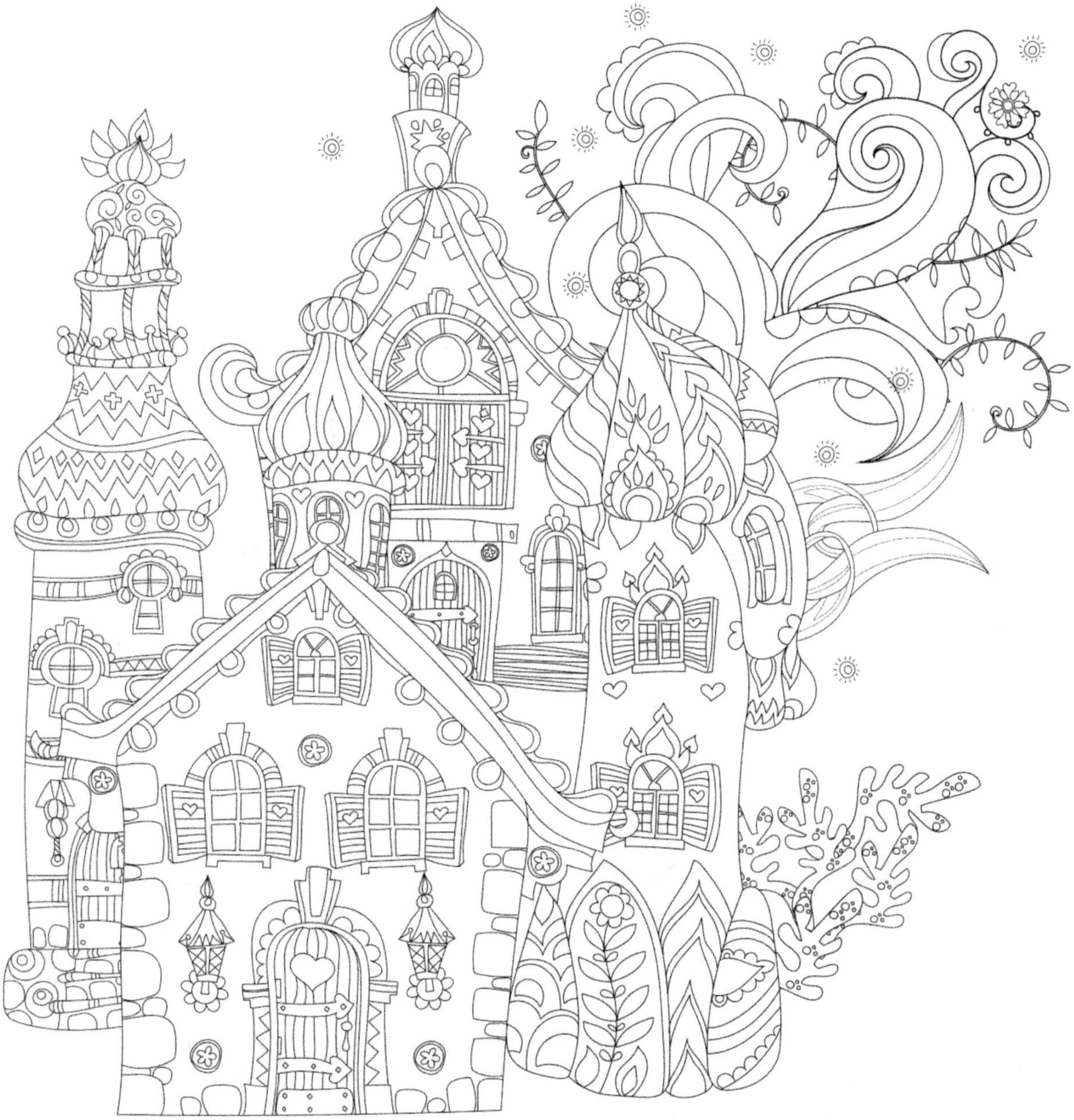

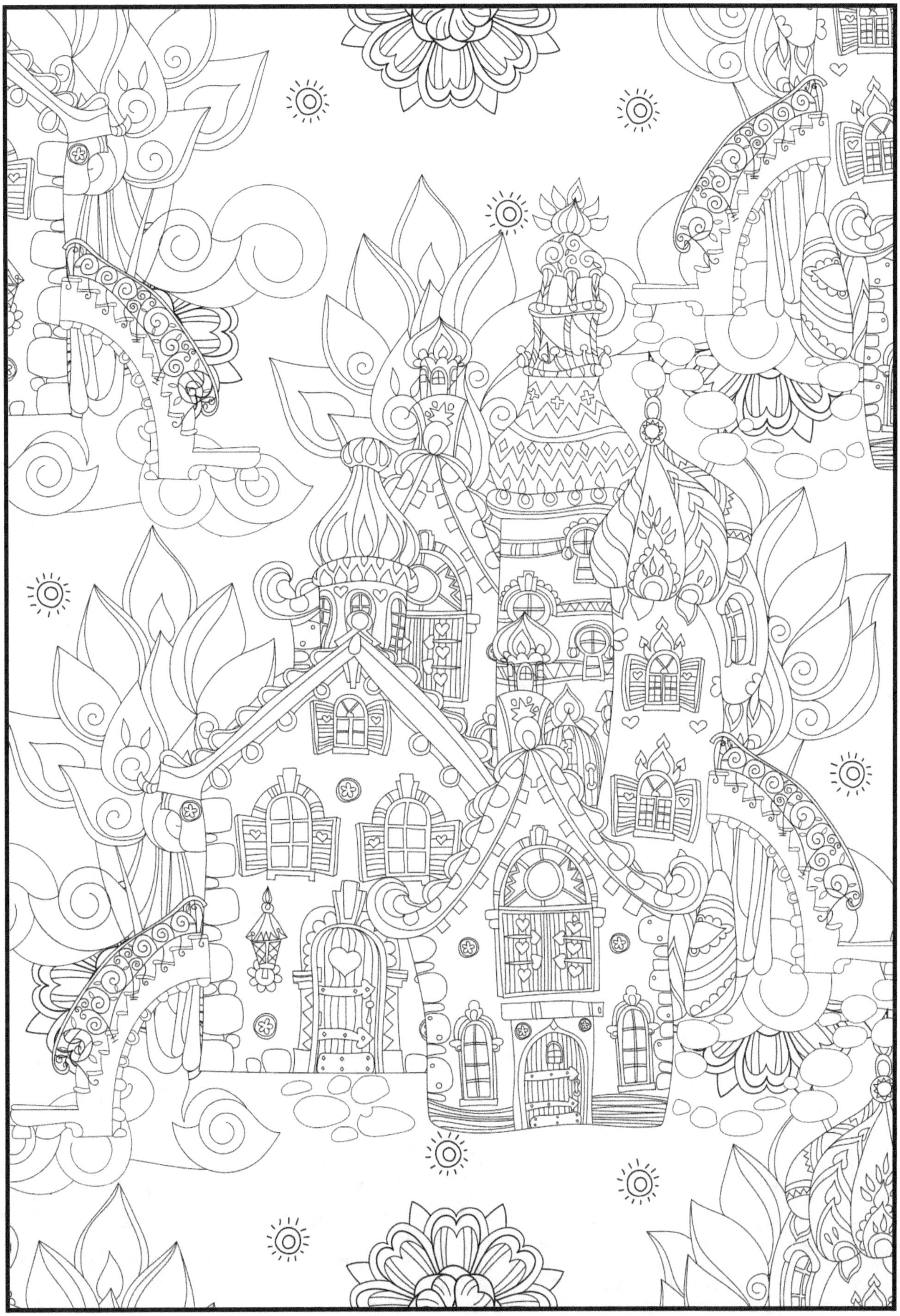

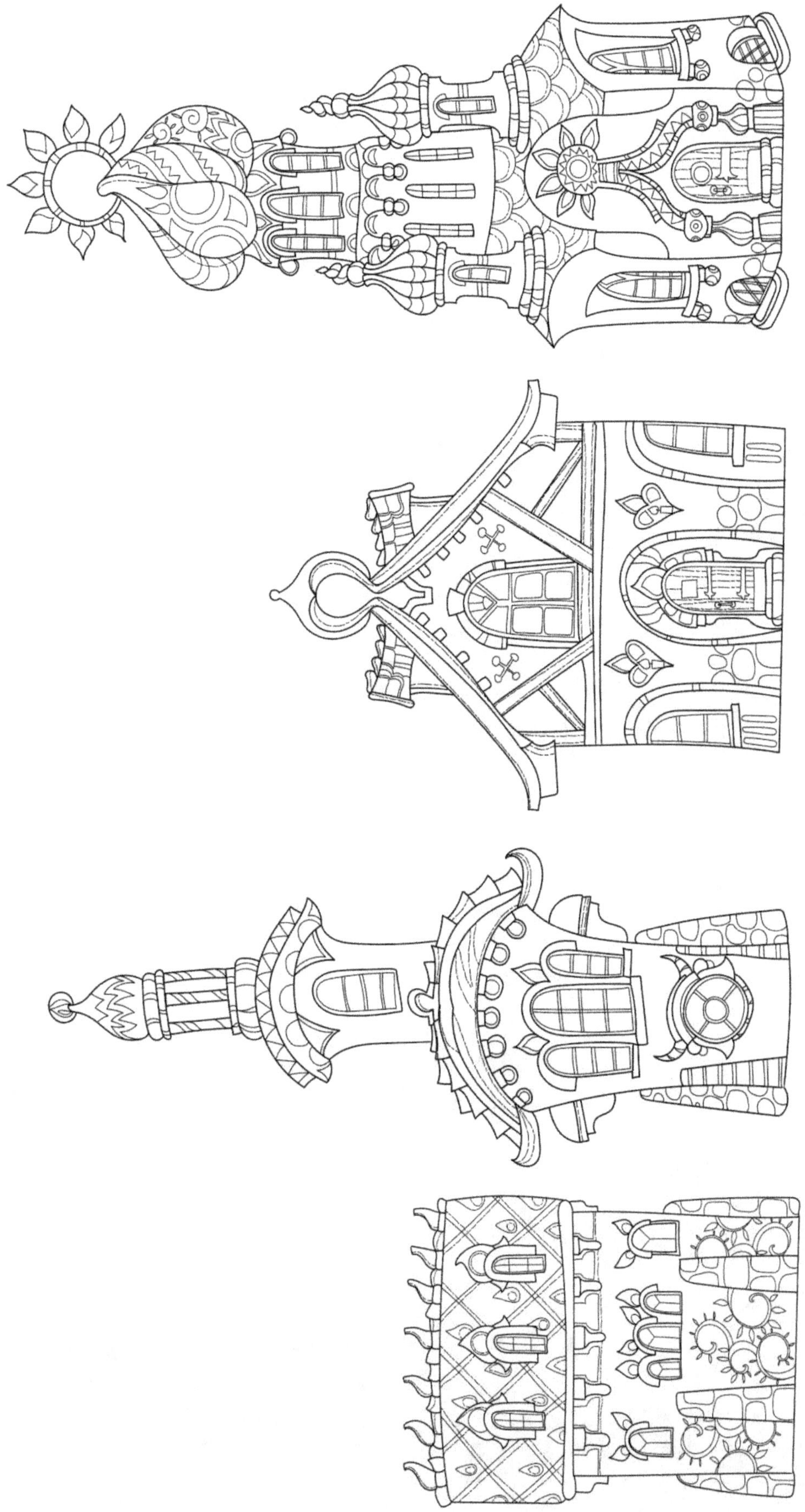

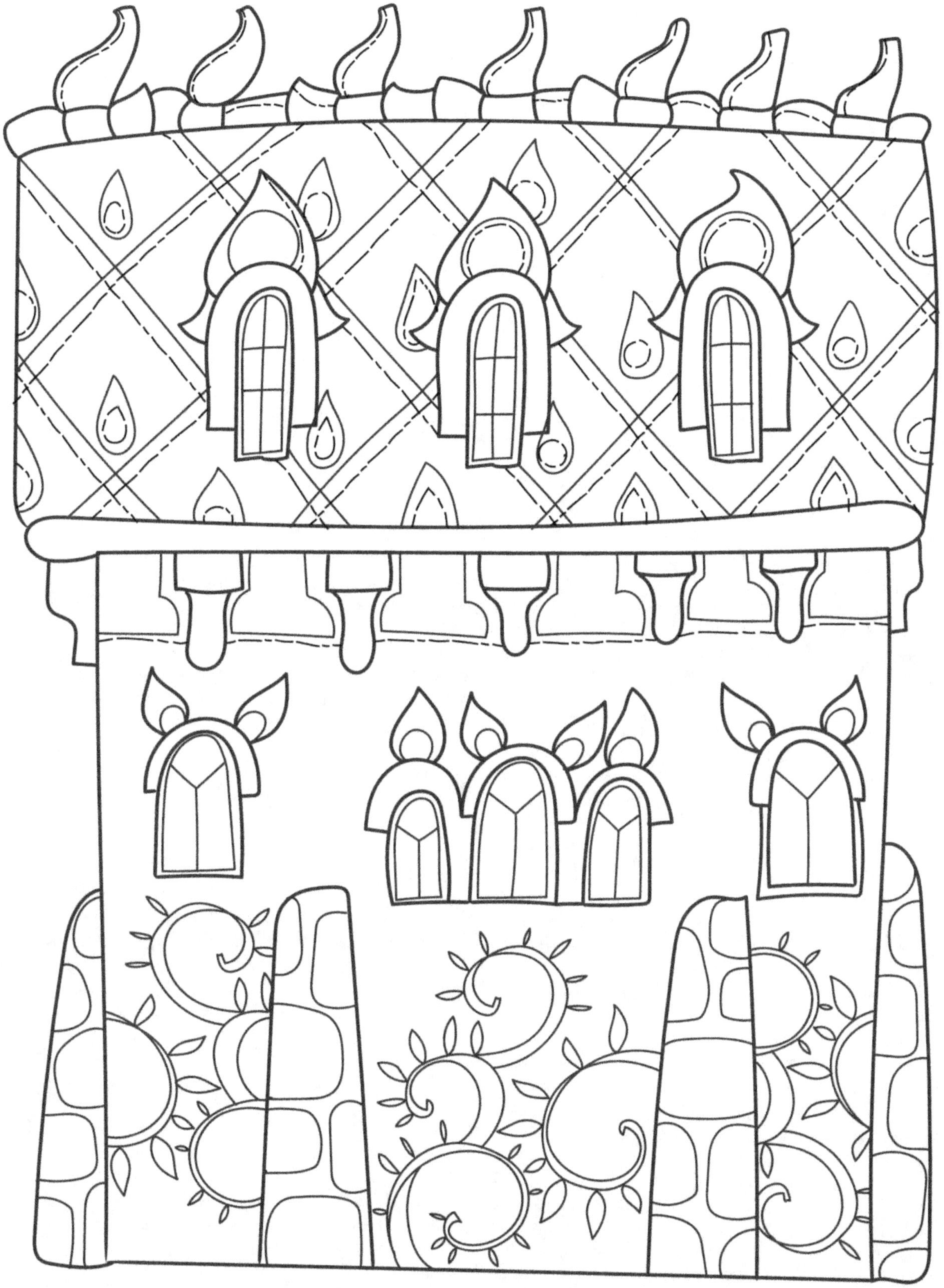

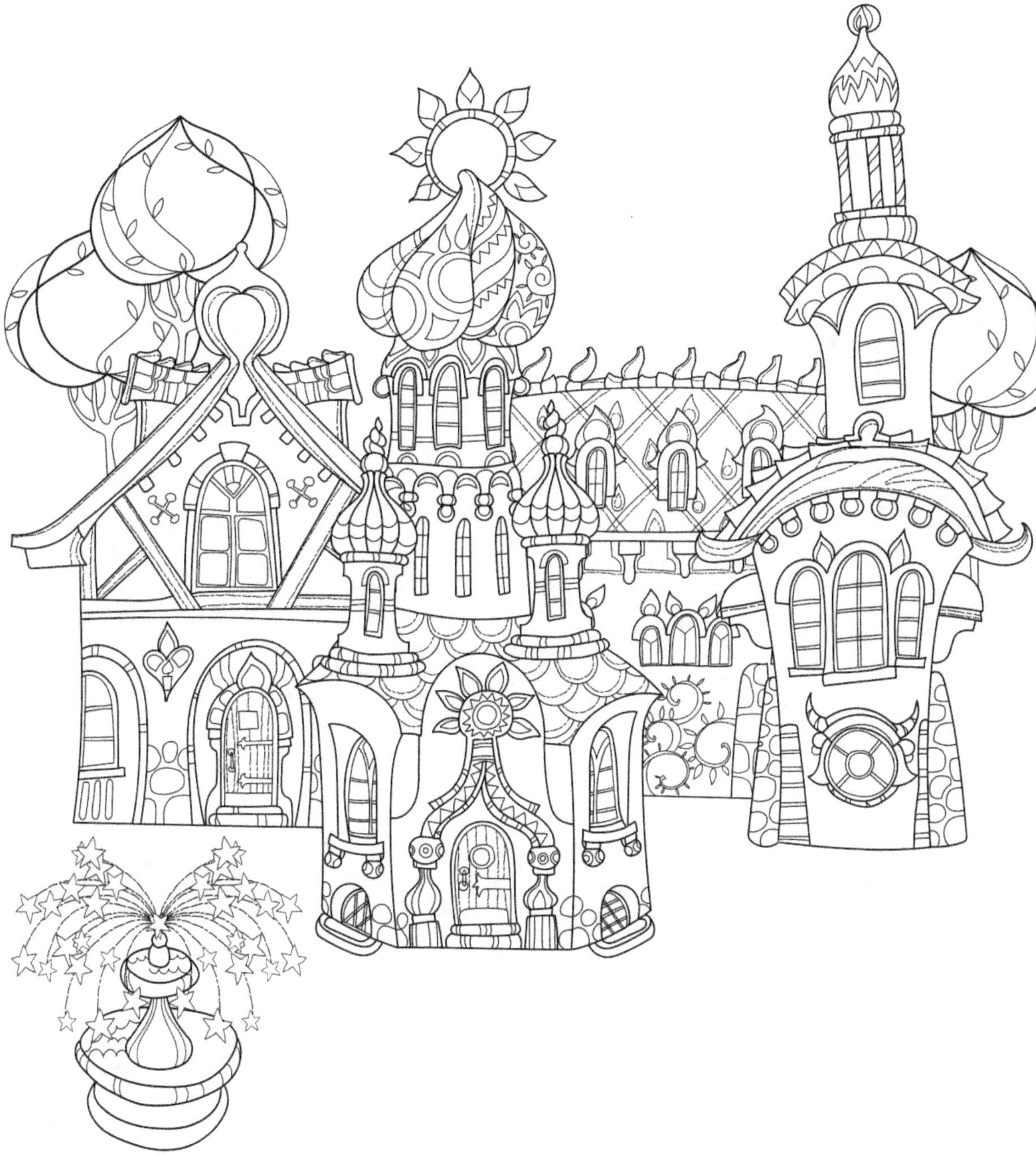

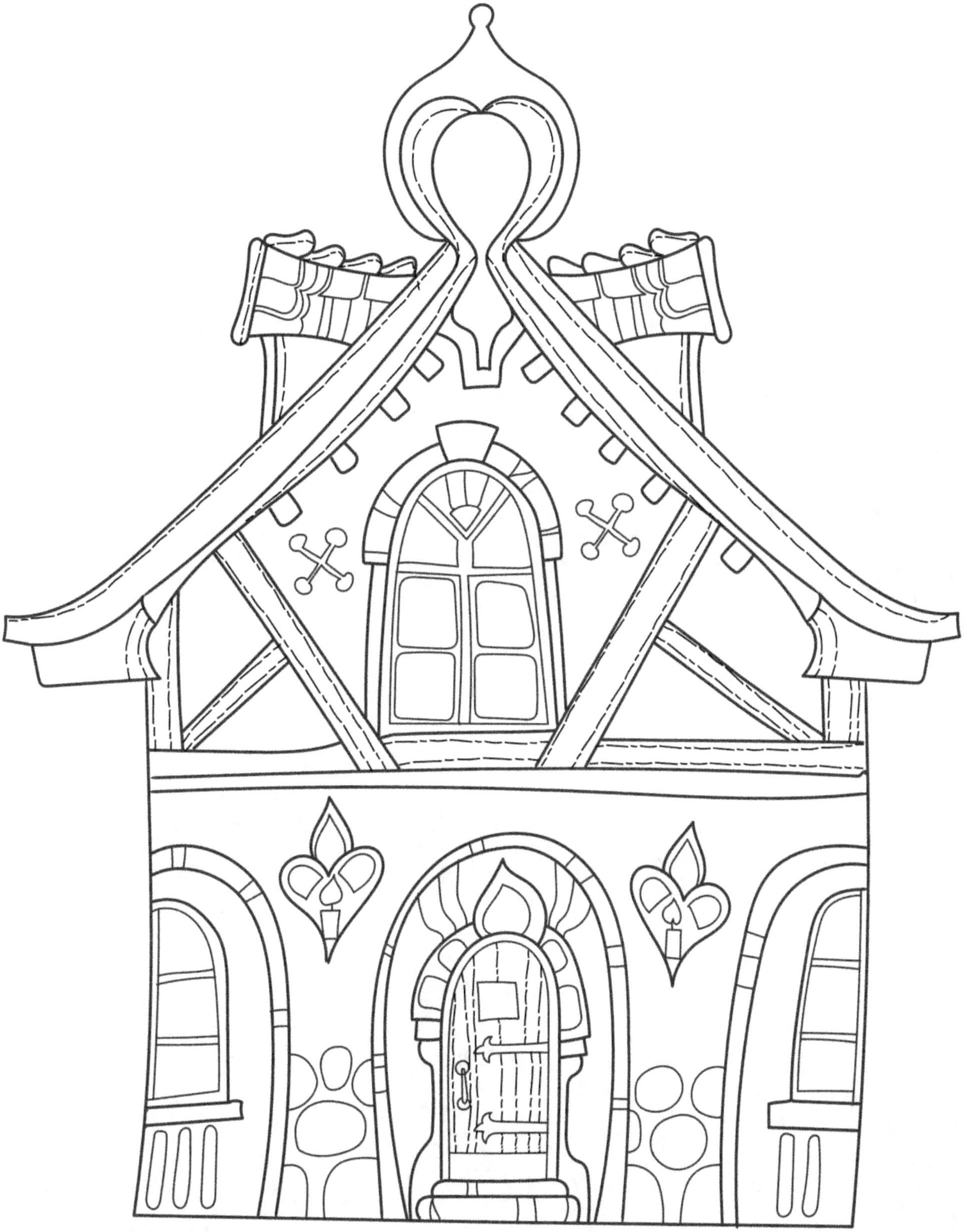

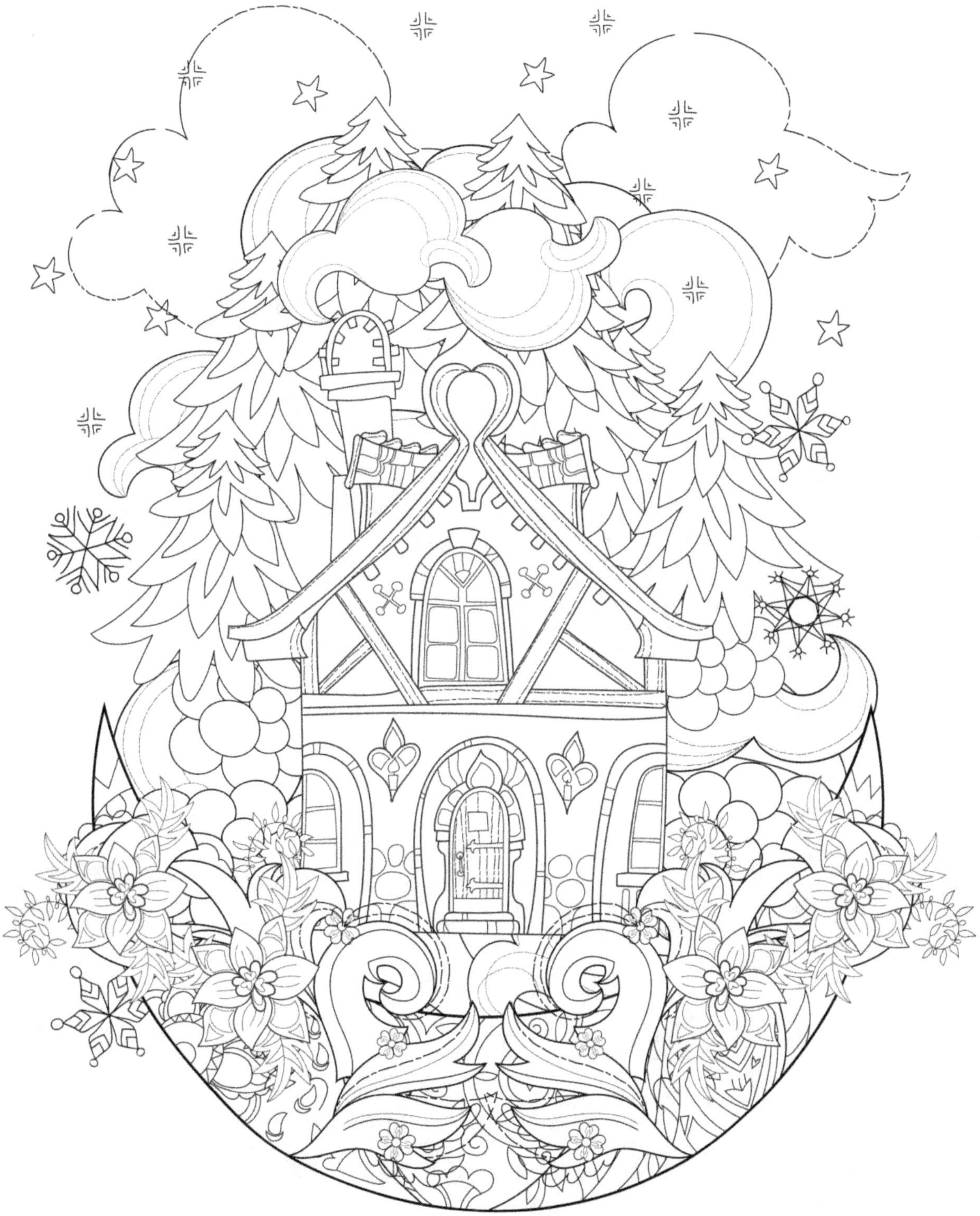

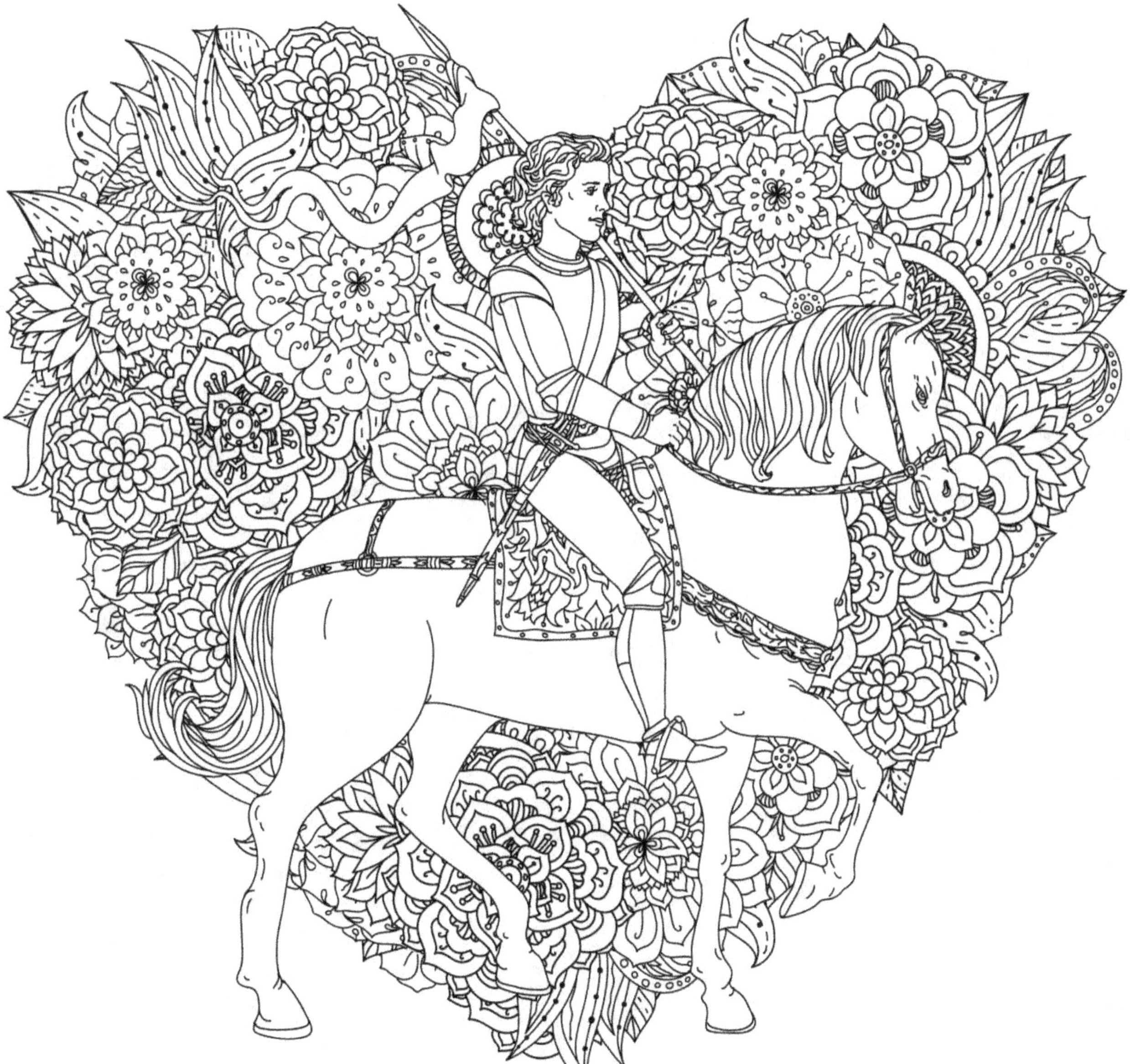

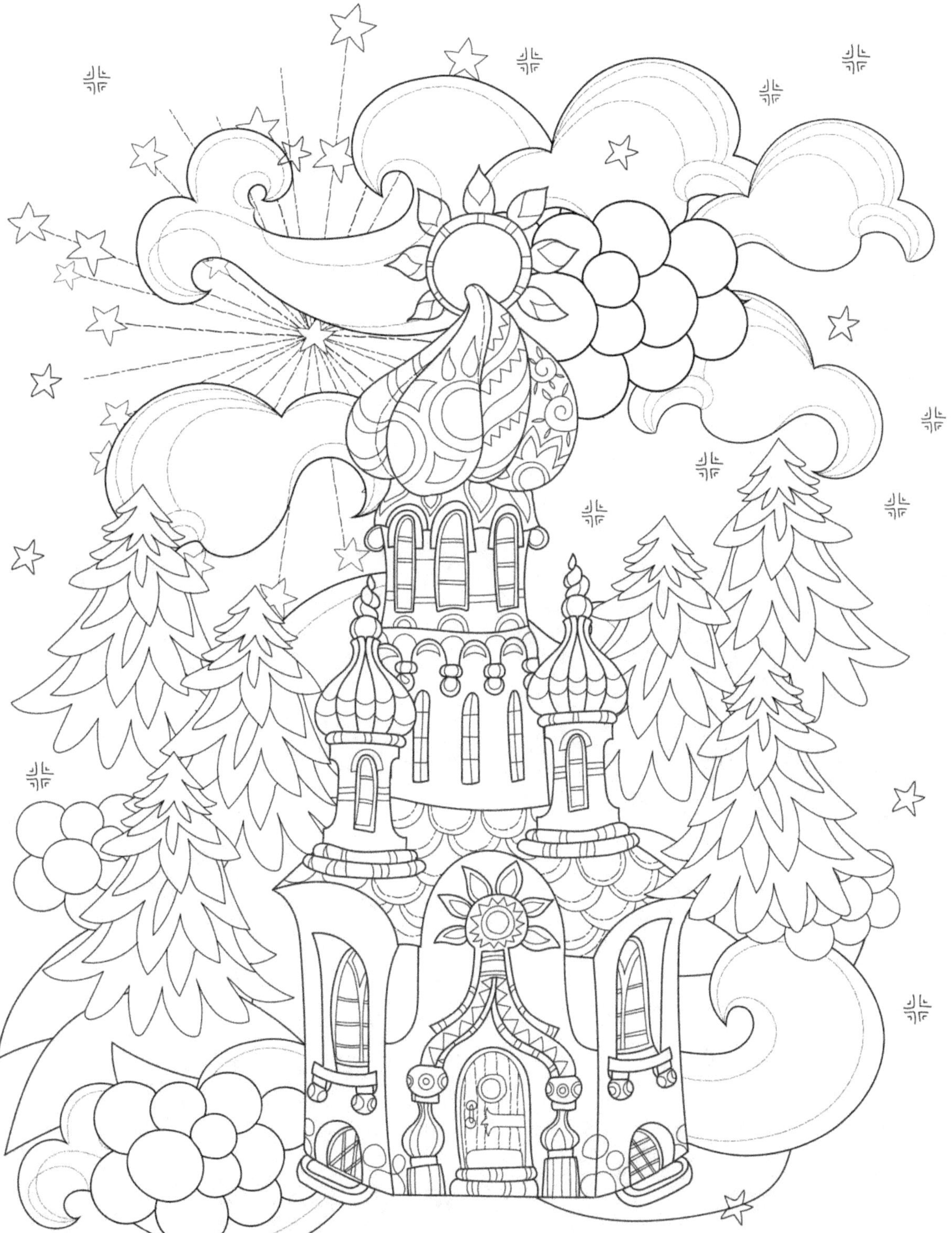

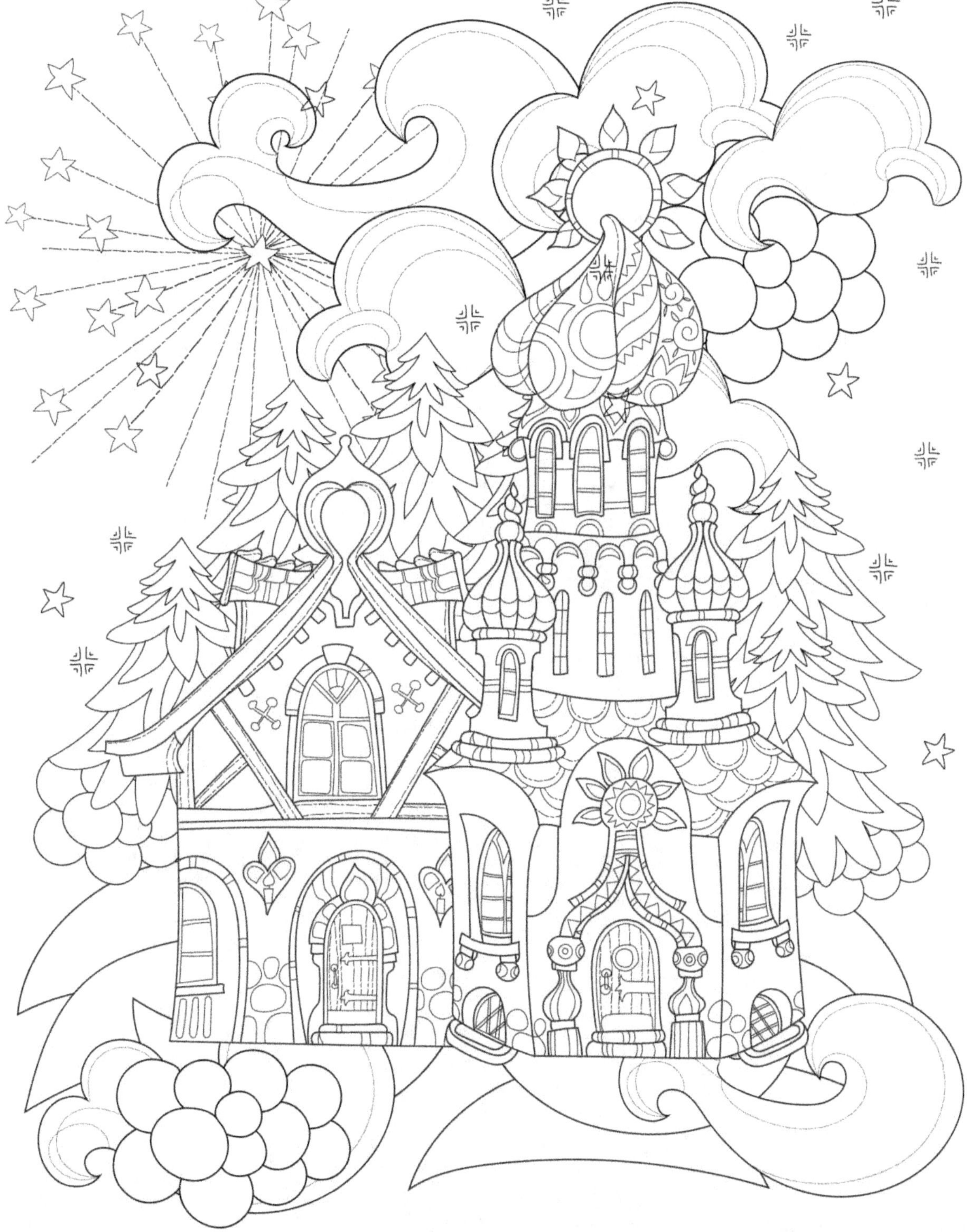

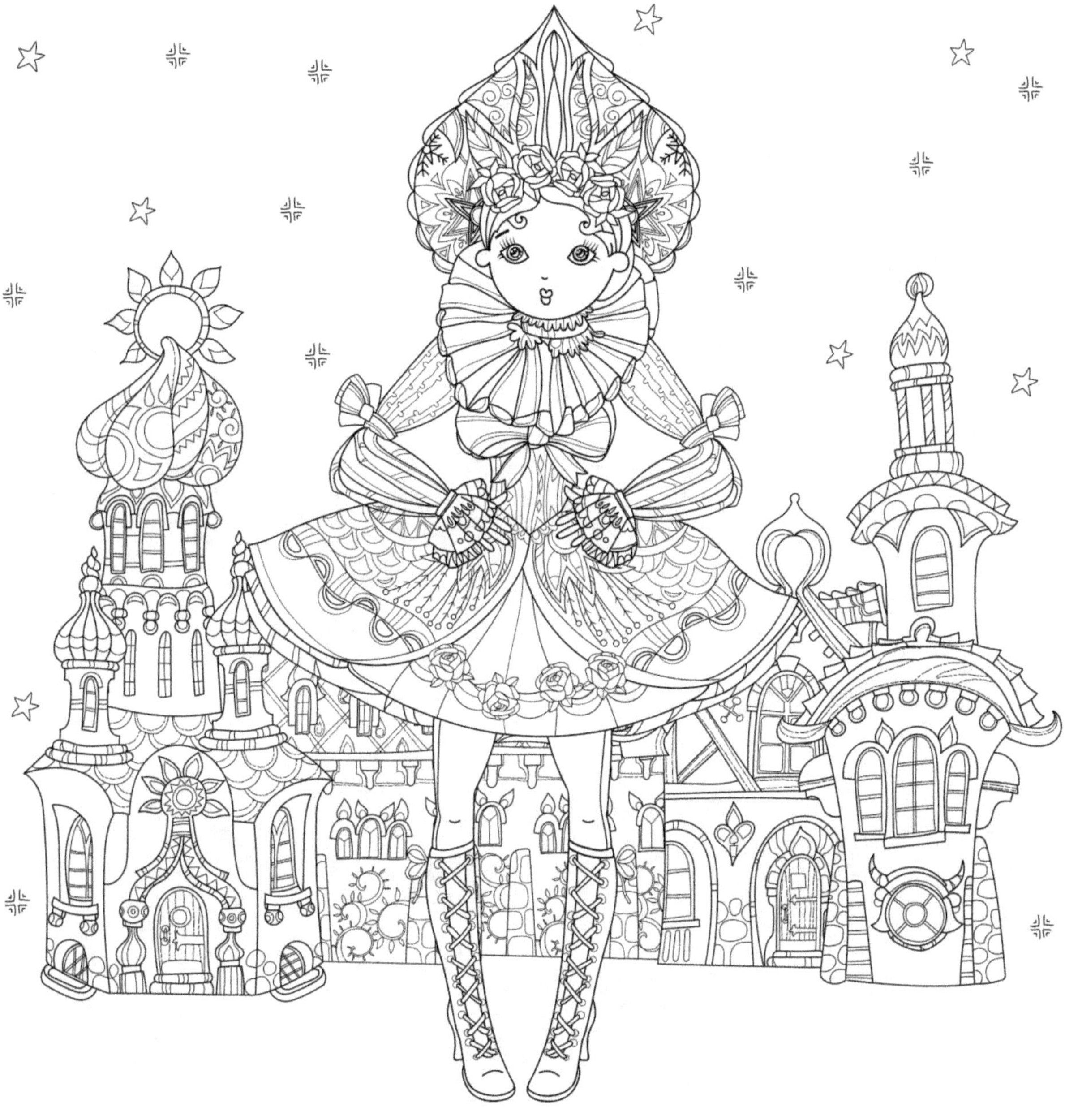

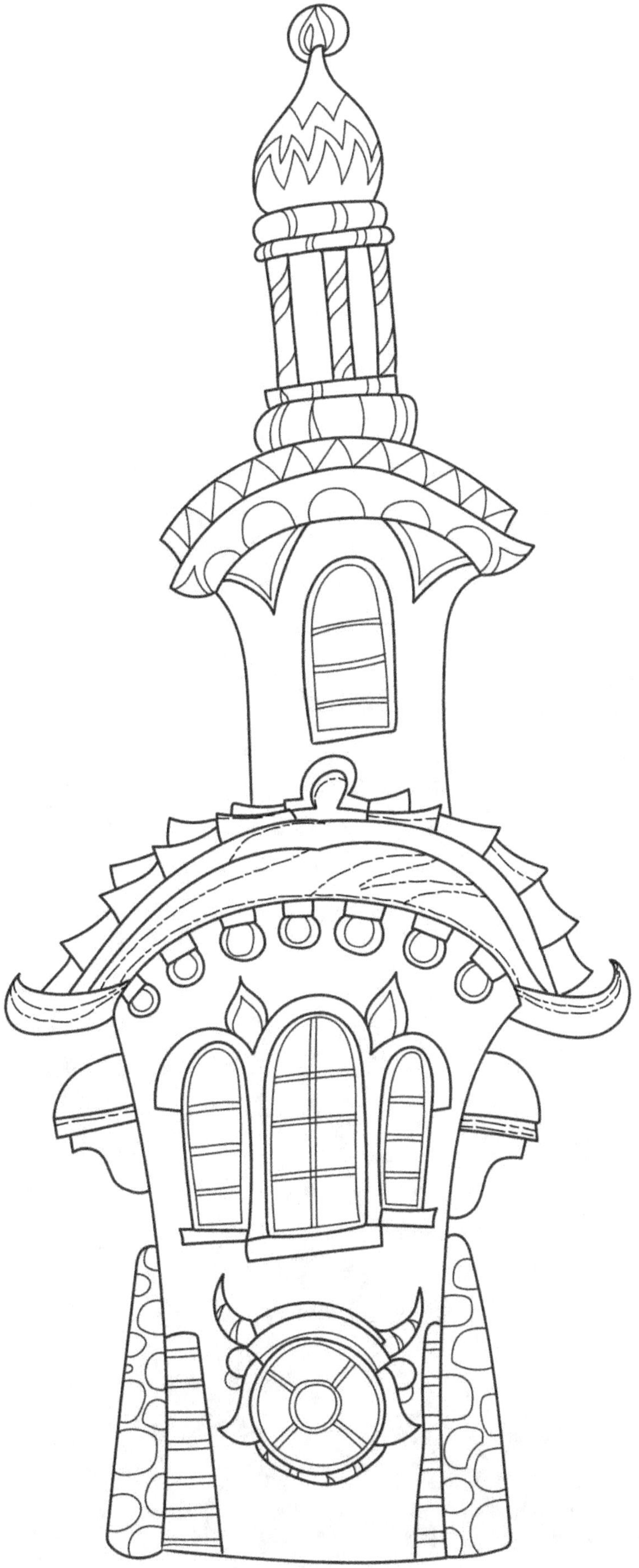

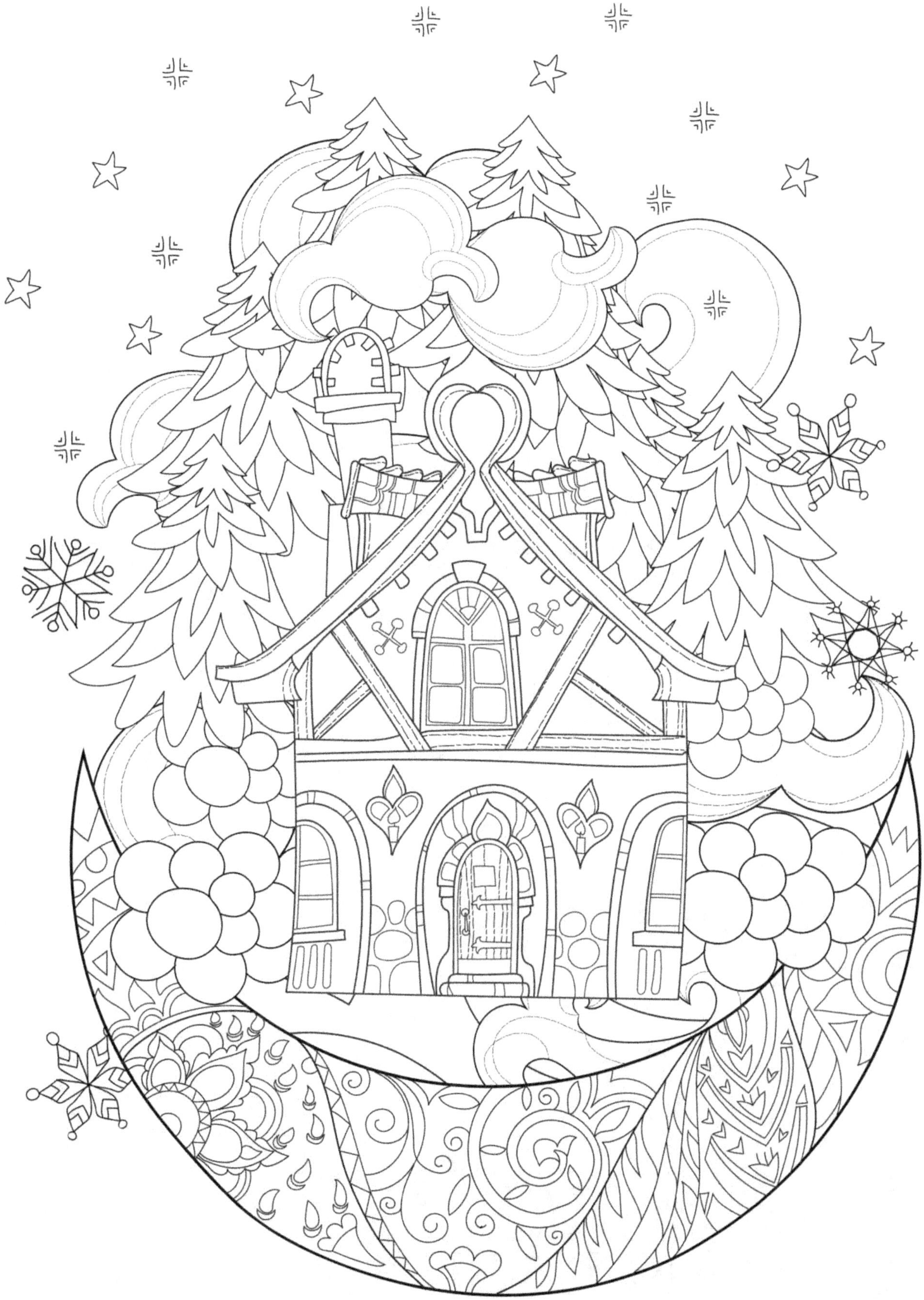

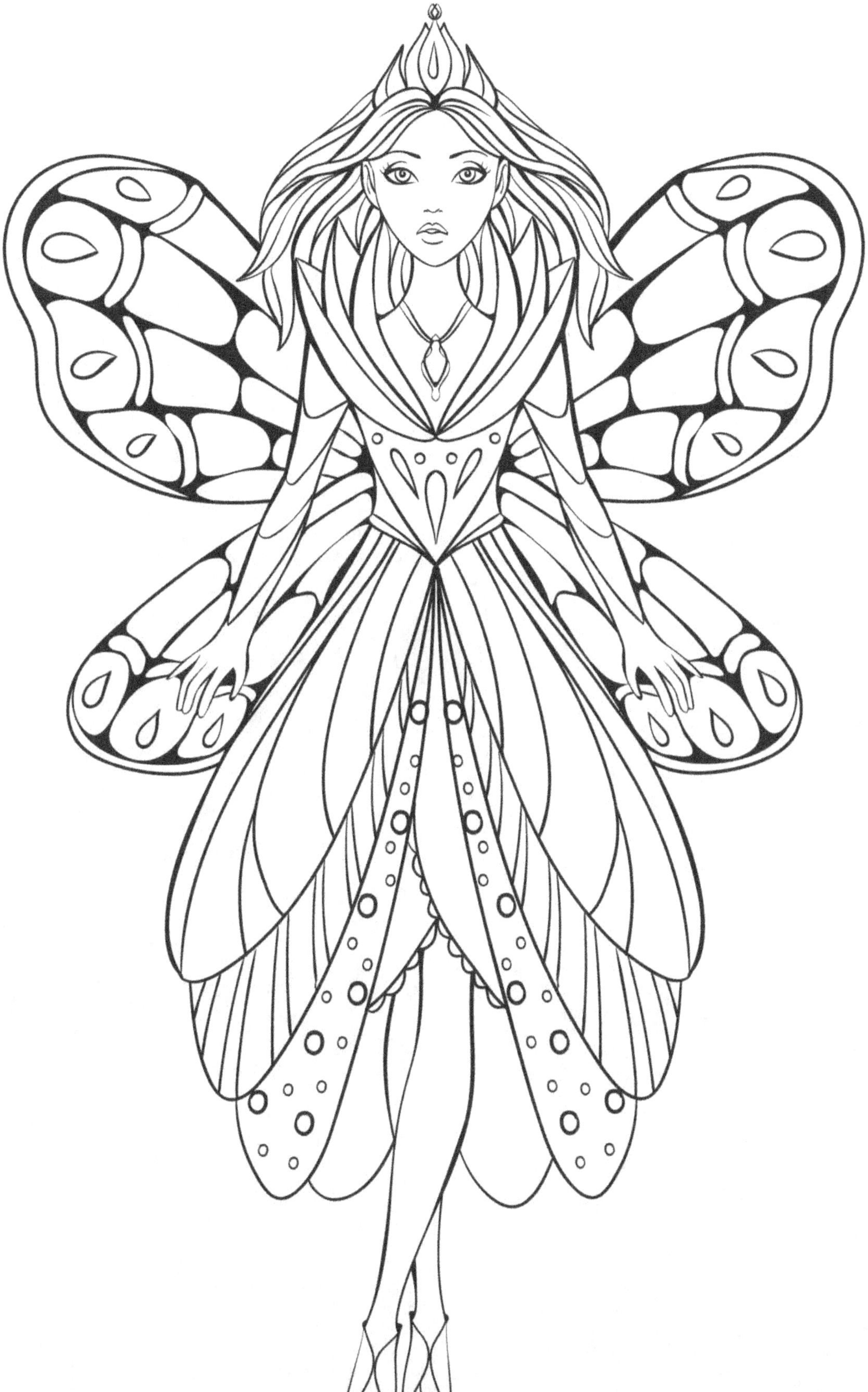

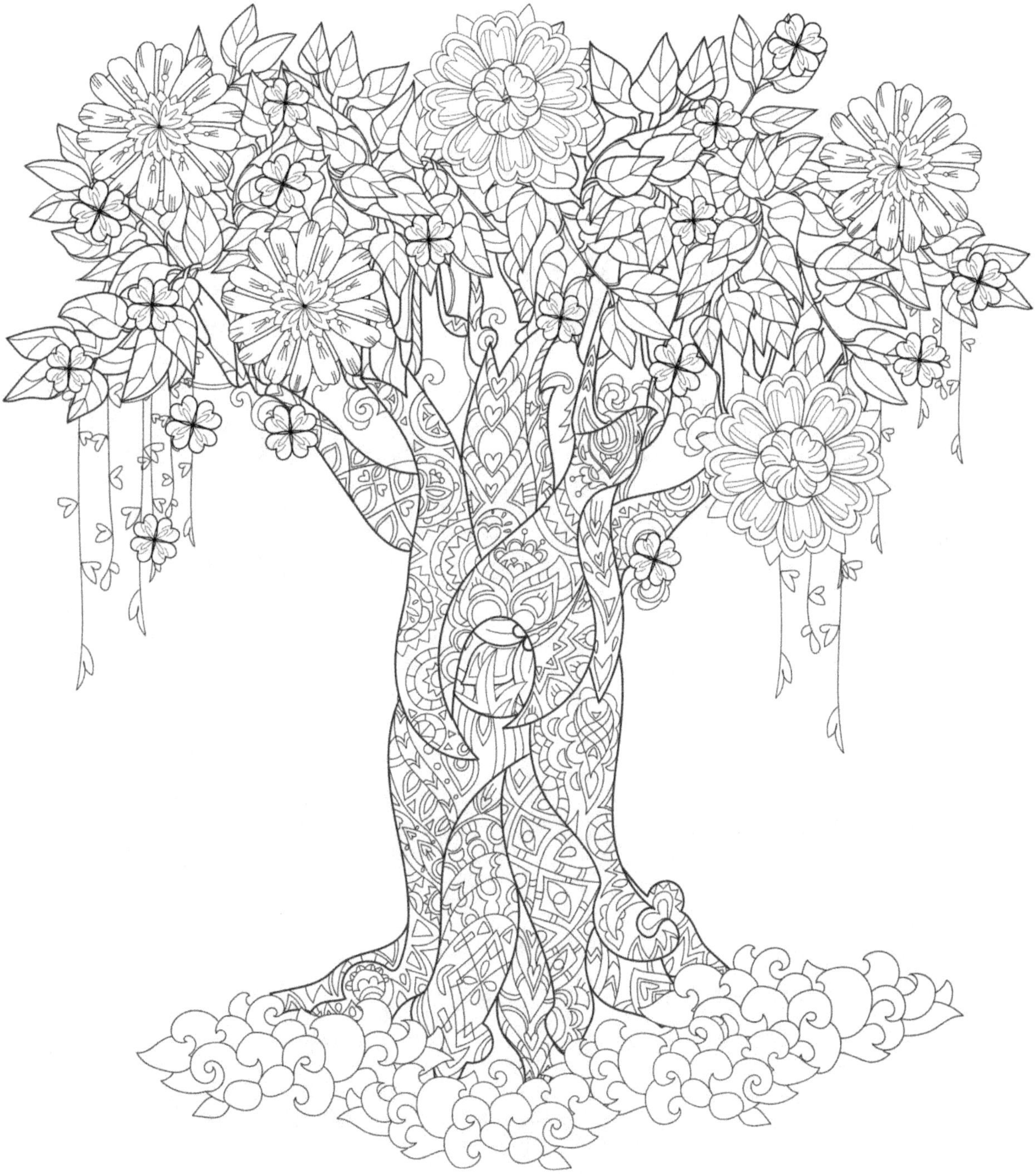

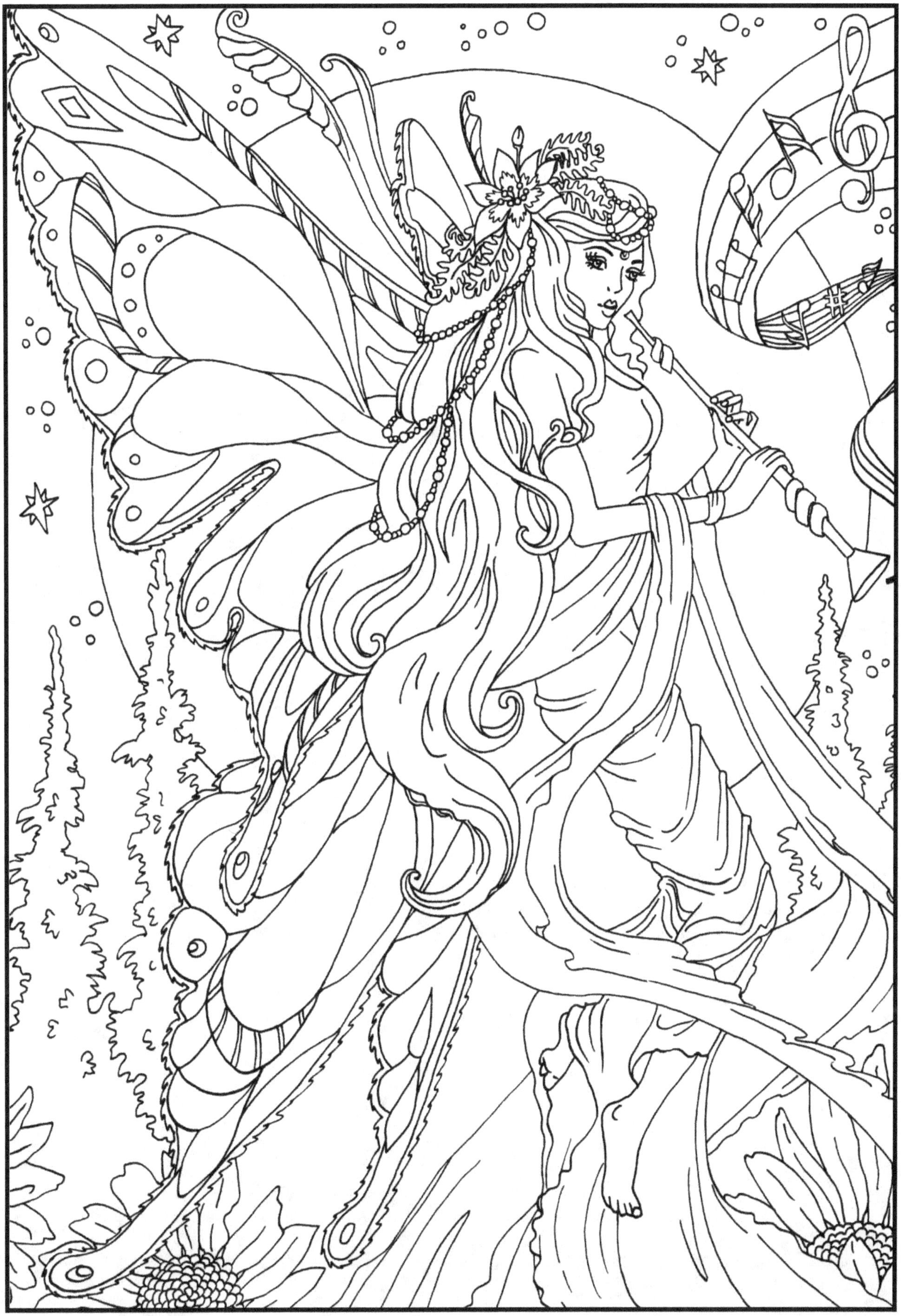

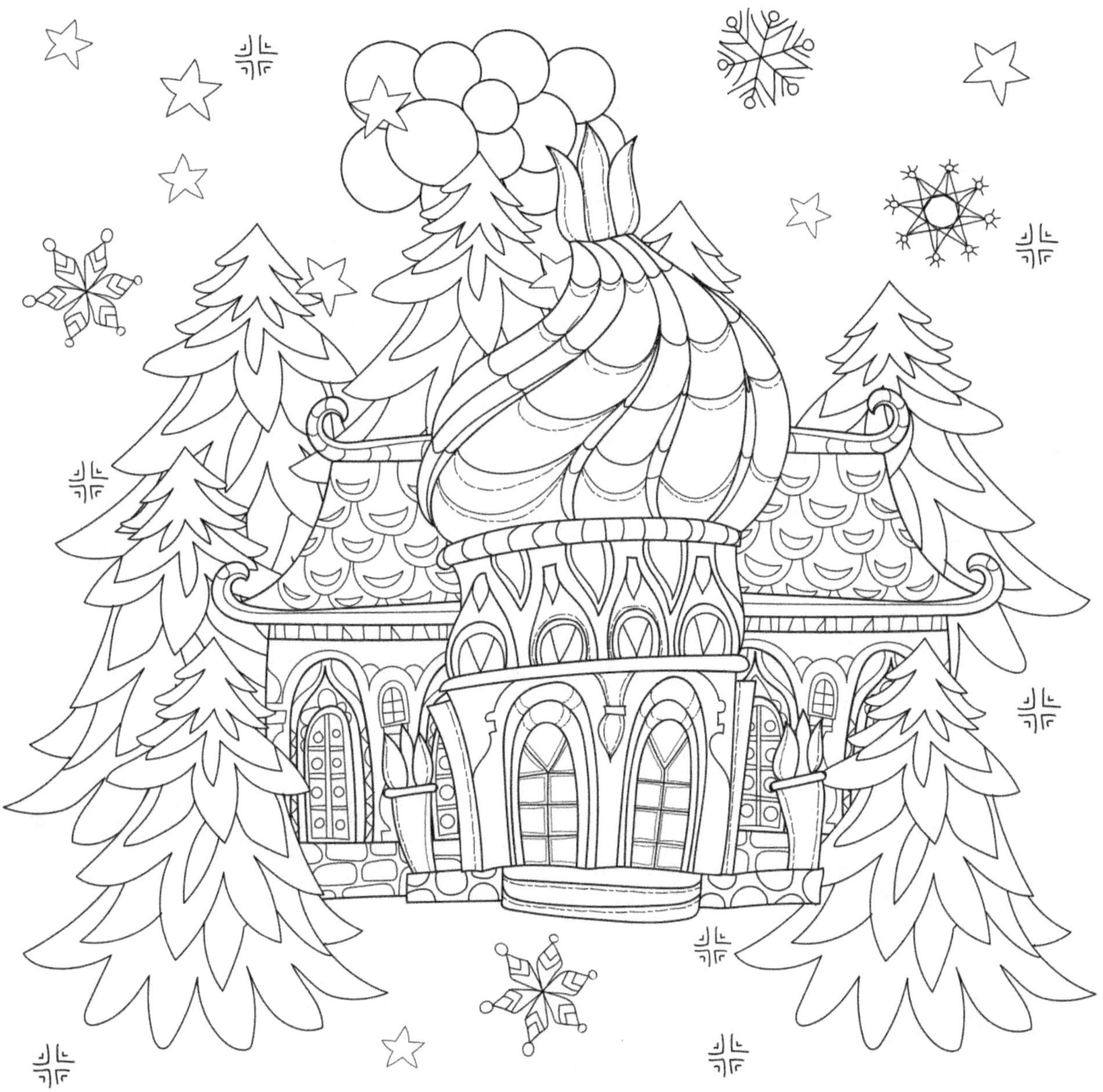

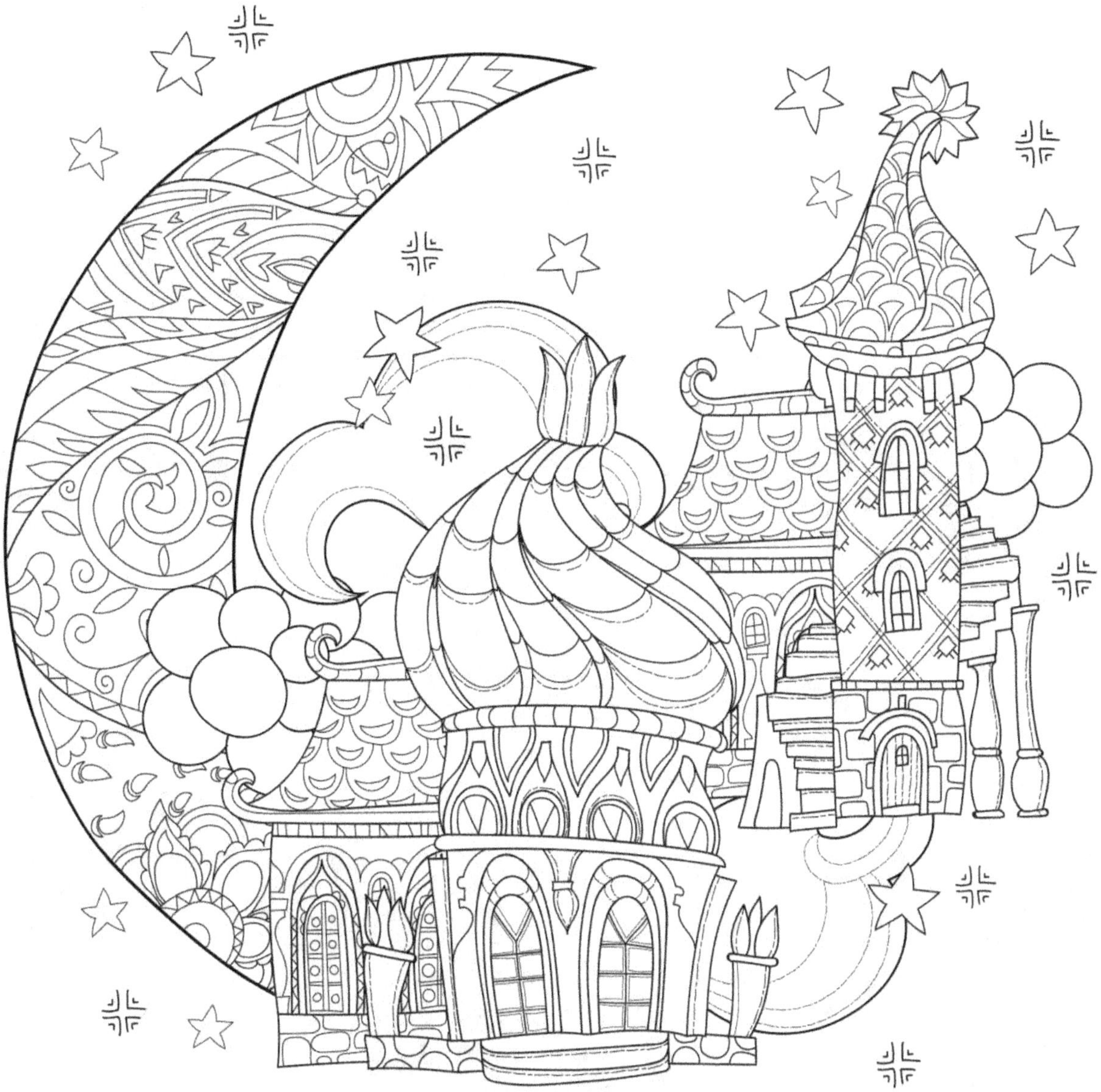

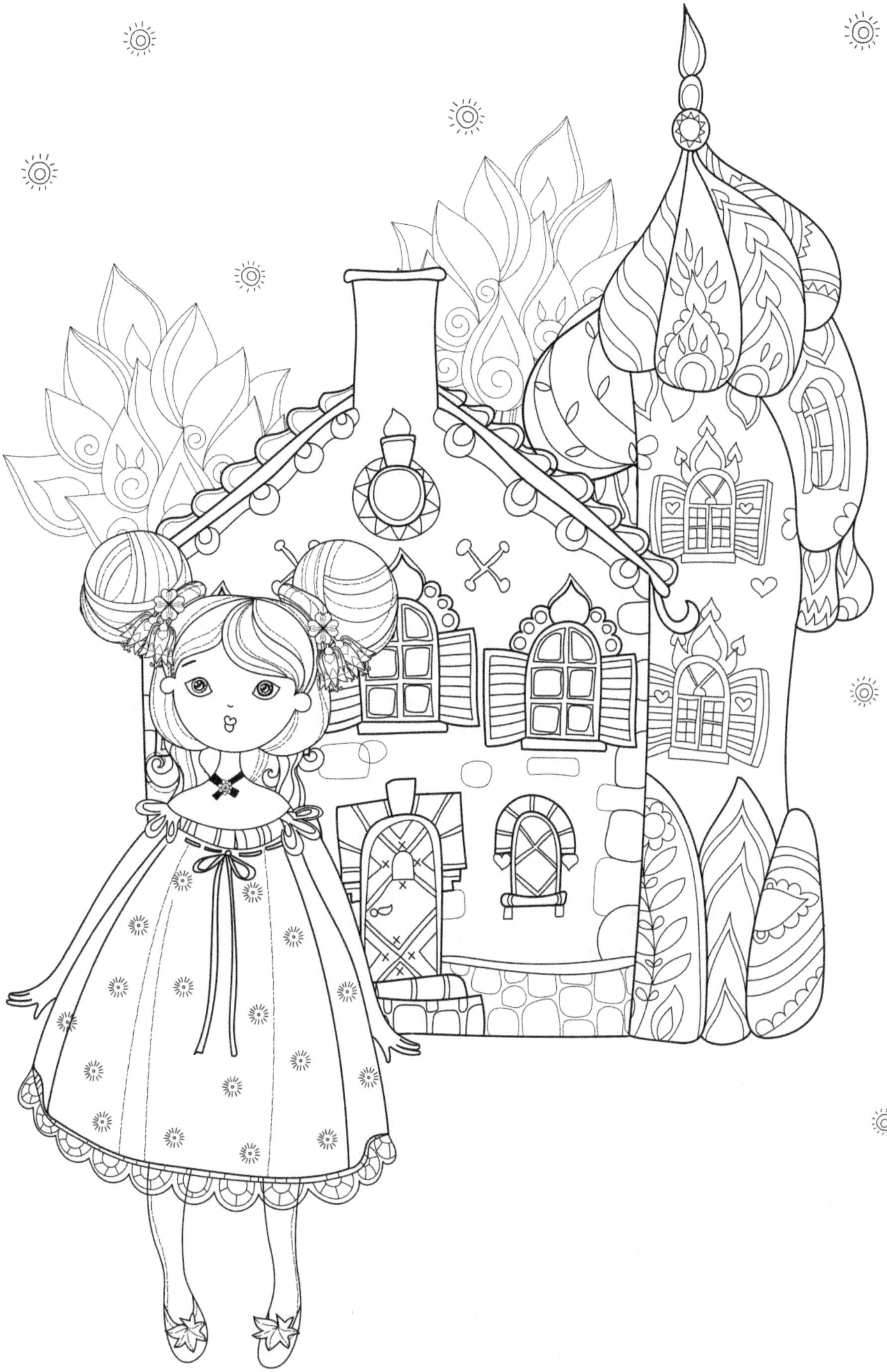

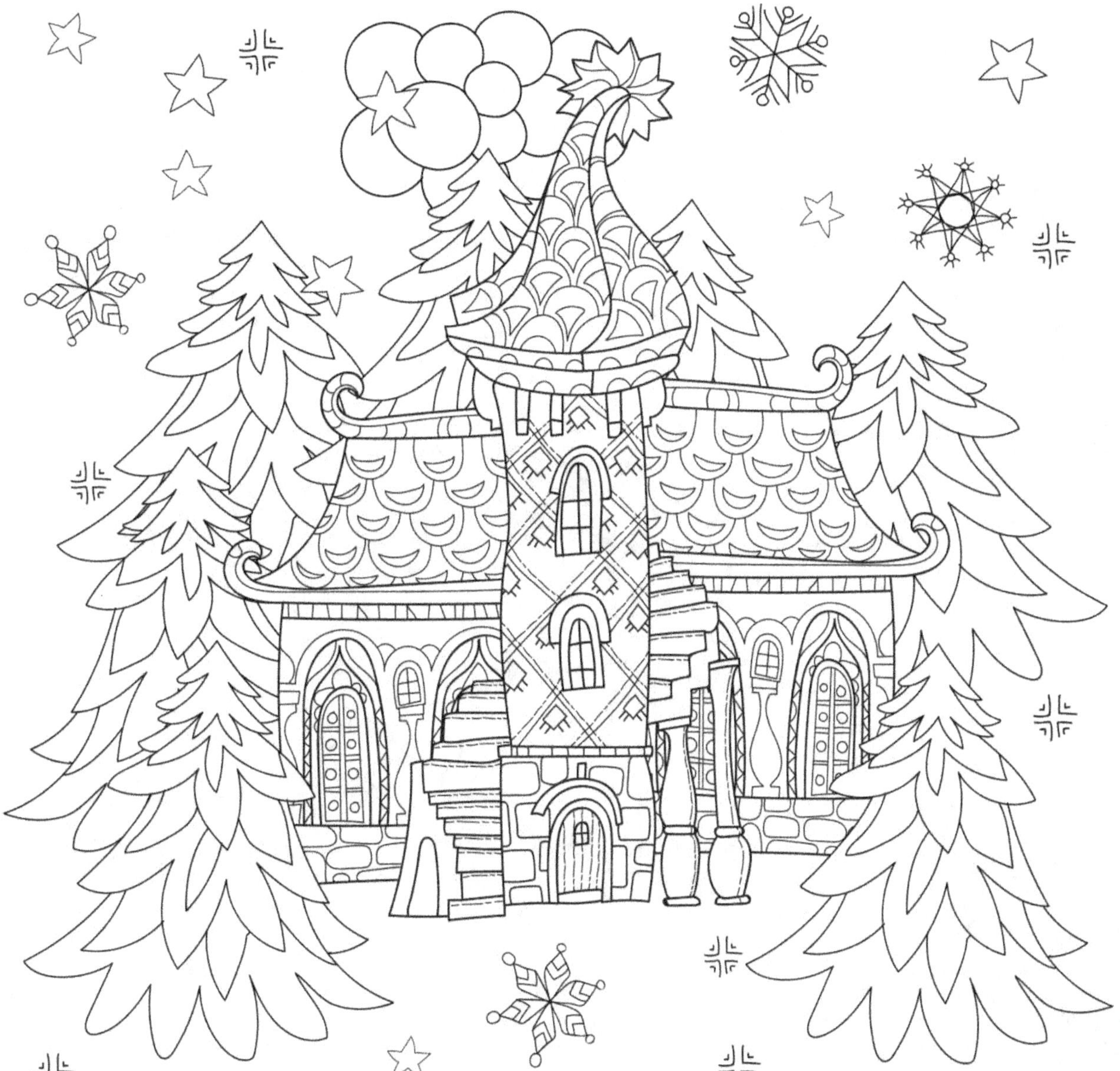

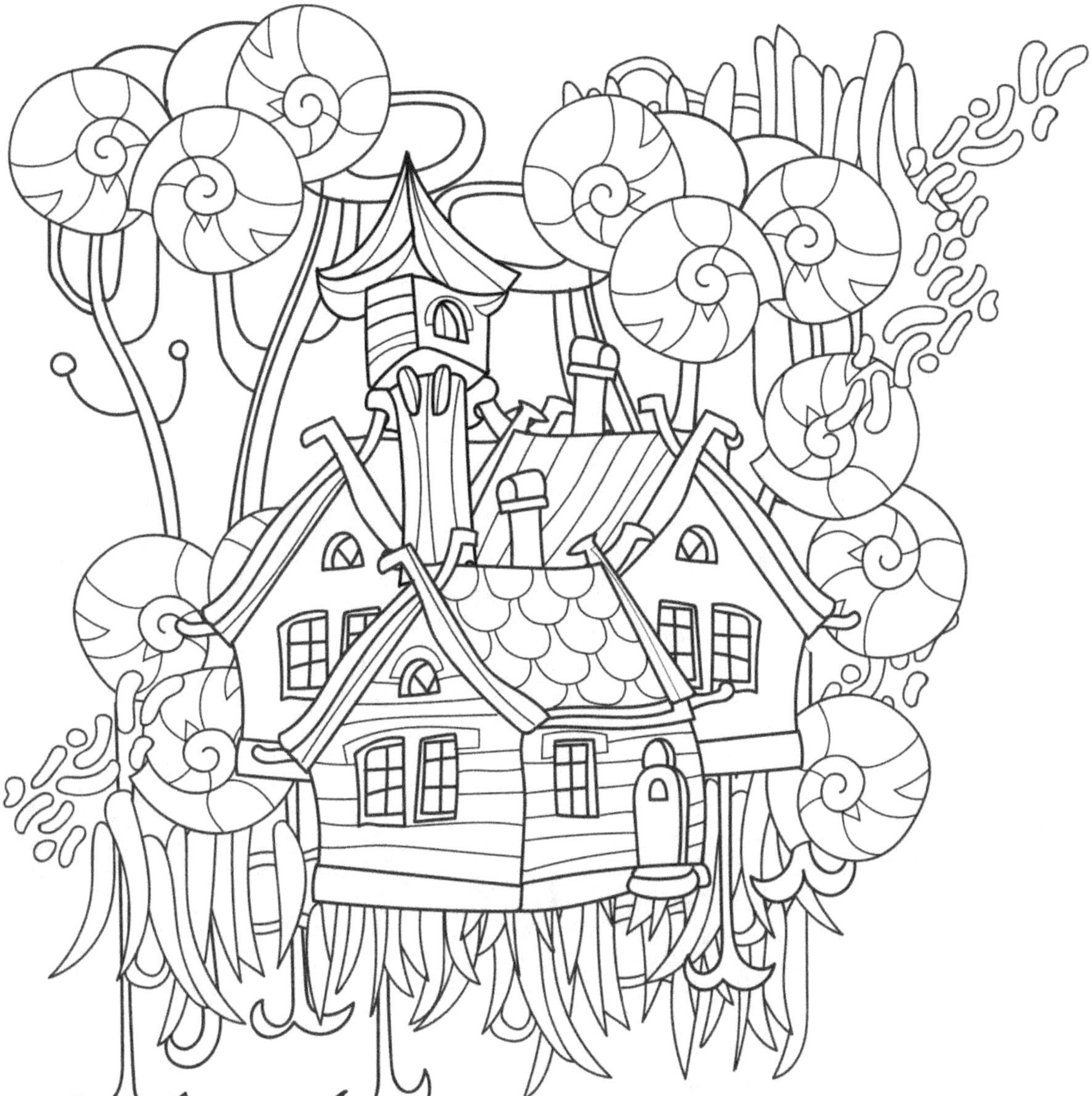

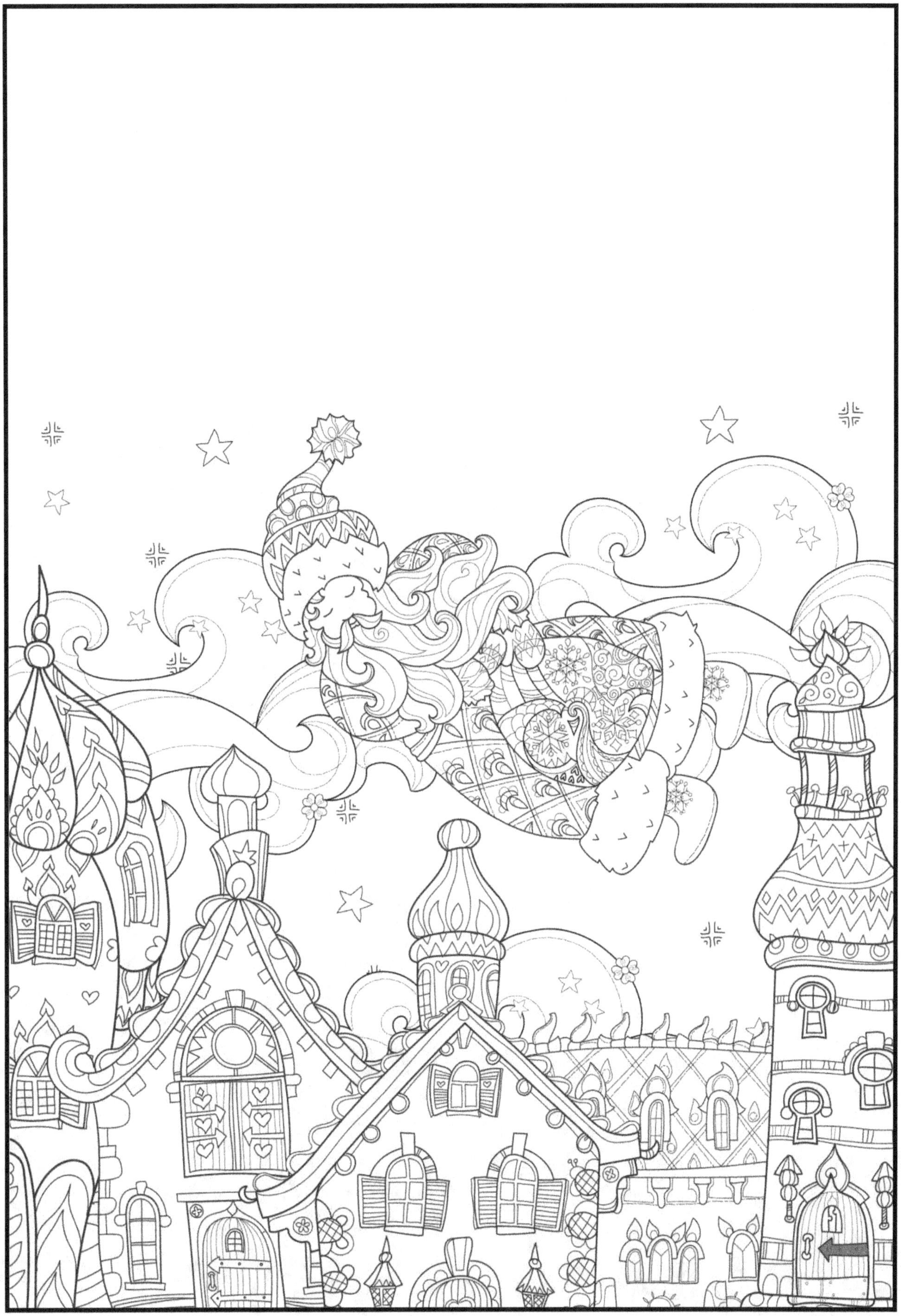

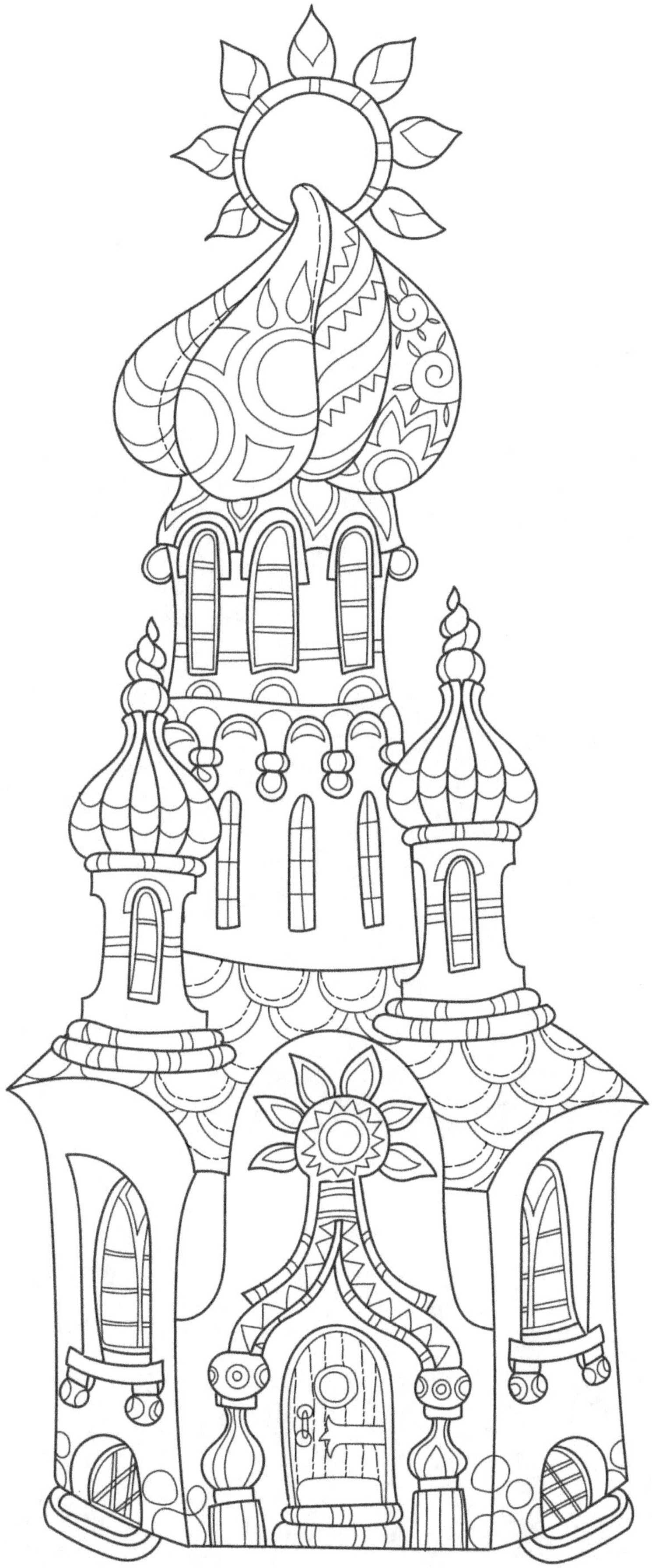

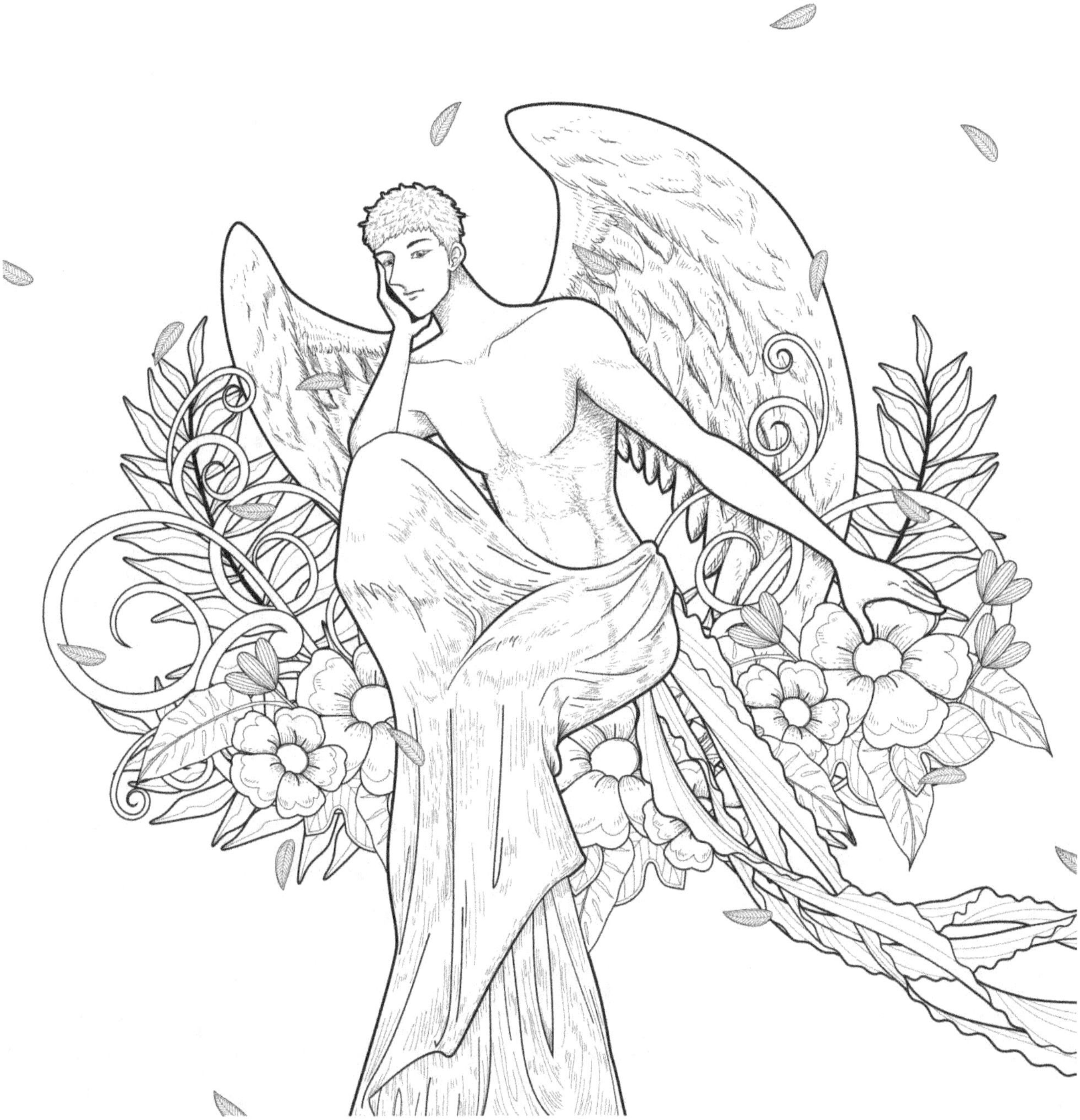

www.ingramcontent.com/pod-product-compliance
Lightning Source LLC
Chambersburg PA
CBHW081258180526
45170CB00007B/2477
* 9 7 8 1 5 4 1 2 1 2 7 0 1 *